MARGRET & H.A. REY'S
Curious George's
Favorite Places

Curious George Goes to the Zoo © 2011 by Houghton Mifflin Harcourt Publishing Company
Curious George Visits a Toy Store © 2002 by Houghton Mifflin Harcourt Publishing Company
Curious George Goes to a Chocolate Factory © 1998 by Houghton Mifflin Harcourt Publishing Company

hmhbooks.com
The text was set in Garamond.
The illustrations were done in watercolor and black colored pencil.

ISBN: 978-0-358-16902-4
paperback

Manufactured in China
SCP 10 9 8 7 6 5 4 3 2 1
4500791378

D1302888

Houghton Mifflin Harcourt • Boston New York

MARGRET & H.A. REY'S
Curious George
Goes to the Zoo

Written by Cynthia Platt

Illustrated in the style of H. A. Rey by Mary O'Keefe Young

This is George. George is a good little monkey and always
very curious. Today, George was feeling very excited.
The man with the yellow hat was taking him to the zoo!

As they drove, the man explained to George that this wasn't just any zoo that they were going to visit.

"It's called the Wild Animal Park," the man said. "All of the animals roam around freely."

When they arrived, George saw a huge
banner. George looked up at it, but he
could not read the words.

A friendly zookeeper explained.

"It's an extra-special day here at the Wild Animal Park," she said. "It is our baby rhino's first birthday. We are going to have a party for her later on!"

A party! This was going to be a wonderful trip to the zoo.

George tried to walk into the park where the animals were, but the zookeeper stopped him.

"You can't walk in there!" she said.

"To explore this zoo, you have ride in one of our special cars."

She pointed to a huge car that had no roof on it.

Oh, my! What fun this was going to be.

George and his friend climbed onboard and the car drove into the park.

Soon they were in the midst of the Wild Animal Park.

"Look over there!" said the zookeeper. "There's our pride of lions. We have a large family here."

George pointed in the other direction. "Yes, George," said the zookeeper. "I see the giraffes, too. Their tall necks help them eat leaves from the tree-tops. And there are two ostriches running this way!"

George was happy to be seeing so many amazing animals.

The zoo car drove past a small pond. Pink flamingos waded in the water. Their heads bobbed up and down as they walked on spindly legs.

"The flamingos turn pink because they eat so many tiny pink shrimp," said the zookeeper, but George was not listening.

He had never seen flamingos before. He was curious about how those flamingos were moving.

He leaned out the back of the zoo car as far as he could to take a look. But then—oh! What happened?!

First George lost his balance. Then he fell—*kerplunk!*—right out of the zoo car. His friend hadn't noticed that he had fallen. George ran as quickly as a little monkey could toward the pond.

The flamingos bobbed their heads and lifted their feet one at a time. It looked like they were dancing. George danced with them.

Suddenly, the water in the pond started to move. Then a hippo popped its head out from under the water. What a surprise! George stopped dancing to take a look.

The hippo opened its huge mouth as if it were yawning. George opened his mouth wide, too. It was fun to act like the hippo!

Just then, George noticed that something was rustling in the reeds near the pond. George was curious. He wanted to see what was there.

In an instant, he jumped over to the reeds. He poked his nose inside and saw . . . a baby rhino!

The tiny rhino was cute, but she looked a little
bit sad and a little bit lonely.

George wanted to make that
baby rhino feel happy again.
He thought and thought.
Maybe the baby rhino would
like the flamingo dance.

He jumped and bobbed
his head and danced his
feet up and down.

The baby rhino peeked her head out of the reeds so that she could watch. George danced more, and the rhino walked out of the reeds.

She was curious, too!

They were having so much fun that George didn't notice what was behind him.

The zookeeper stomped over to George. She did not look happy. The man with the yellow hat was running behind her.

"You are a naughty little monkey," said the zookeeper. "You were supposed to stay in the car. You and your friend will have to go now."

George walked to the man's side. He waved goodbye to the baby
rhino. The man and the zookeeper turned to see whom George was
waving to.

"The baby rhino! Why, we've been looking for her all day," said
the zookeeper. "She got separated from her mother."

George was glad to see the zookeeper looking happy again. He and the man started walking toward the exit.

The zookeeper ran to stop them. "Thank you for finding our baby rhino, George. And just in time for her birthday party. Will you join us for some cake?"

George jumped with glee. He had forgotten about the party, and he did love cake.

The man and George followed the zookeeper and the baby rhino back to zoo headquarters. The rhino's mother was waiting there for her.

The zookeeper brought out a special birthday cake that was shaped like a rhino. George had never seen a cake like that before.

"You can have the first piece, George," said the zookeeper. "I also have a special treat, just for you!" She placed a bunch of bananas in front of him.

George was very happy to have a tasty banana, but he saved room for some cake, too!

MARGRET & H.A. REY'S

Curious George
Visits a Toy Store

Illustrated in the style of H. A. Rey by Martha Weston

This is George.

He was a good little monkey and always very curious.

Today was the opening of a brand-new toy store. George and the man with the yellow hat did not want to be late.

When they arrived, the line to go inside wound all the way around the corner. When a line is this long, it's not easy for a

little monkey to be patient. George sneaked through the crowd.
All he wanted was a peek inside.

George got to the door just as the owner opened it.
"This is no place for a monkey," she said.

But George was so excited he was already inside!
Balls, dolls, bicycles, and games filled the shelves.

There were so many toys —

George didn't even know
how some of them worked.

And how about these hoops?
What did they do?
   George was curious. He climbed
up to pull one out of the pile.
   It would not move.
   George pulled harder.
   Still it wouldn't move.
   George pulled with all fours.

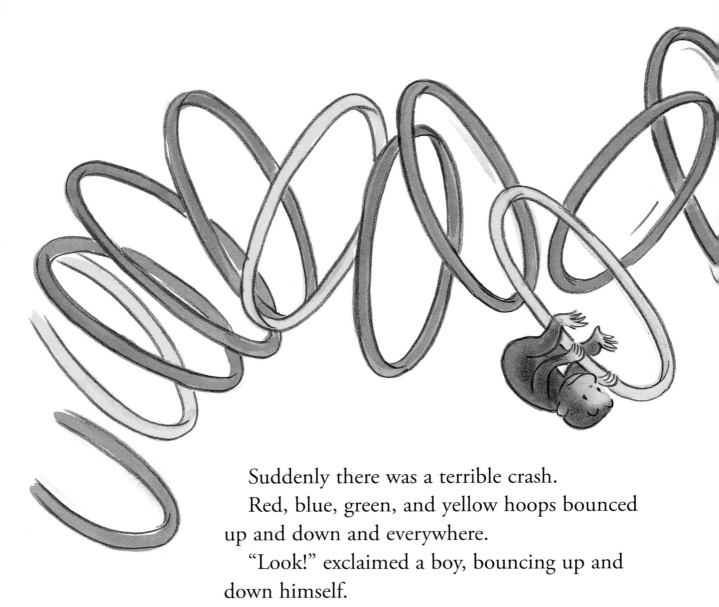

Suddenly there was a terrible crash.

Red, blue, green, and yellow hoops bounced up and down and everywhere.

"Look!" exclaimed a boy, bouncing up and down himself.

"Why, I haven't seen one of these in years!" said the boy's grandmother.

She put a hoop around her waist and gave it a spin.
George tried the hula hoop, too!

Then George pretended to be a wheel.

He rolled and rolled and. . . .

Oops! He rolled right into the owner.

The owner shook her head. "I knew you were trouble," she said. "Now you've made a mess of my new store."

Again she tried to stop George.

And again George was too quick.

In only a second he was around the corner and on the highest shelf.

Below him, George saw a
little girl point to a toy out of
reach. "Mommy, can we get that dinosaur?" she asked.

George picked up the dinosaur and lowered it to the girl.

She was delighted. So was the small boy next to her. "Could

you get that ball for me, please?" he asked George.

George reached up, grabbed the ball, and bounced it to the boy.

"May I have that puppet way over there?" asked another girl.

How lucky that George was
a monkey! He swung off the
shelf, hung on to a light, picked
up the puppet, and put it right
into her hands.

"What a show!" shouted a boy.
The children held up their new toys
and cheered. What a commotion!

Immediately the owner came running,
and then came the man with the yellow hat.
  "I think we've had enough
monkey business for one day,"
the owner frowned.

Just then a girl got in the long line to pay. "What a great store," she said. "What a great idea to have a little monkey helping you," her father told the owner.

"I guess you're right," the owner replied, and smiled.
Then she gave George a special surprise.
"Thank you, George," she said. "My grand
opening is a success because of you. Perhaps
monkey business is the best business after all."

The end.

MARGRET & H.A.REY'S
Curious George
Goes to a Chocolate Factory

Illustrated in the style of H. A. Rey by Martha Weston

This is George.

George was a good little monkey and always very curious.

One day George went for a drive with his friend, the man with the yellow hat.

"Look, George," the man said. "There's a store in that chocolate factory up ahead. Let's stop for a treat."

George loved chocolates.
Inside the store, boxes of
chocolates were stacked everywhere, but the man with the yellow
hat found his favorites right away.
"George," he said, "wait here while
I buy these, and please stay out
of trouble."

George looked around the store.
He saw chocolate-covered cherries
and fudge-flavored lollipops.
A chocolate bunny caught his eye.

Then something else caught his eye.
What were all those people looking at?
George was curious.

He climbed up to get
a better look. Through
the window he saw lots
of trays filled with little
brown dots.

What were all those
little brown dots?

George was curious.
He found a door that led
to the other side of the window.

The little brown dots were chocolates, of course! A tour guide was showing a group of people how to tell what was inside the chocolates by looking at the swirls on top.

This little swirl means fudge,

this one says that caramel is inside,

and this wiggle is for marshmallow.

This is the squiggle for a truffle,

this one is for nougat,

this sideways swirl is for orange fluff,

and this one is for George's favorite — banana cream.

George followed the tour group until they came to a balcony overlooking a room where the chocolates were made. Down below, busy workers picked the candy off the machines and put them in boxes.

These were the machines that made the chocolates with the swirls on top! The chocolates came out of the machines on long belts. But how did they get their swirls?

George was curious.

He climbed down from the balcony . . .

and up onto a machine.

George peeked inside.
He was trying to see what
was making the swirls when
all of a sudden . . .

the chocolates began
coming out faster and
faster! They sped by him so
quickly they seemed
to be running on legs
of their own.

"Quick! Bring more boxes!" yelled a man with a tall white hat.

"What happened?" asked another man.

Nobody answered. Nobody knew what had happened and everyone was so busy that no one noticed George.

The workers began to fall behind and the candy began to fall off the end of the belt.

"Save the chocolates!" yelled the man with the tall white hat.

Meanwhile, George saw one of his favorites whiz by. He tried to catch the banana-cream chocolate, but it was too fast!

He chased it to the end of the belt.

At the end of the belt a pile of chocolates was growing taller and taller. George had never seen so many chocolates!

As he searched for the banana cream, he put the others in empty boxes.

George was a fast worker. Someone noticed and yelled, "Bring that monkey more boxes! He's helping us catch up!"

Not all the chocolates made it into boxes, but no more chocolates fell on the floor.

Just when George and the workers were all caught up, the tour guide ran in with the man with the yellow hat. "Get that monkey out of here!" she yelled. "He's ruining our chocolates!"

"But this little monkey SAVED the chocolates," explained the workers.

Then the man with the tall white hat said to George, "You may have caused us some trouble, but you were a speedy little monkey. You deserve a big box of candy for all your help."

George was glad he was not in trouble, but he did not take the chocolates.

Back in the parking lot, the workers waved good-bye as George and his friend got into their little blue car.

"George, are you sure you don't want any chocolates before we leave?" asked the man with the yellow hat.

George was sure.